D0400296

Anxious Music

Anxious Music

poems

April Ossmann

James Edgar
and
Jean Jessop Hervey
Point Loma Branch Library

Four Way Books
Tribeca / New York City

Distributed by
University Press of New England
Hanover and London

Copyright © 2007 by April Ossmann. All rights reserved.

No part of this book may be used or reproduced in any manner
without written permission except in the case of brief quotations
embodied in critical articles and reviews. Please direct all inquiries to:

Editorial Office
Four Way Books
POB 535, Village Station
New York, NY 10014
www.fourwaybooks.com

Library of Congress Cataloging-in-Publication Data

Ossmann, April.
Anxious music : poems / April Ossmann.
    p. cm.
ISBN-13: 978-1-884800-81-8 (pbk. : acid-free paper)
ISBN-10: 1-884800-81-5 (pbk. : acid-free paper)
I. Title.
PS3615.OS636A84 2007
811'.6--dc22
2007019422

Cover design: K.C. Witherell / Hello Studio.

This book is manufactured in the United States of America. Four Way Books
is a not-for-profit literary press. We are grateful for the assistance we receive
from individual donors, public arts agencies, and private foundations.

This publication is made possible with public funds from
the New York State Council on the Arts, a state agency.

NYSCA

Distributed by University Press of New England
One Court Street, Lebanon, NH 03766

[clmp]

We are a proud member of the Council of Literary Magazines and Presses.

Table of Contents

One

I wanted the avocados—
I didn't want the avocados.
I wanted something
that cost too much, that
felt too smooth
on my tongue,
that would torment me
with its absence as it would
with its presence.
I never passed them
with indifference. Imagine—
all those weeks
I wanted avocados
and told no one!
I wanted anything
I couldn't have
or perhaps to become one
with the culture
of wanting,
in a world of want.
One united body
of cells fused
with desire, the moving
target perhaps of another's
desire—the potential
right arm of the right man.
Wanted and wanting,
united, I steered my cart
down the market's
gleaming avenues, one
with this nation of desire,
with the luxury, to want.

Epergne

I am looking for *epergne* when I find it, Sunday morning

    in my *Webster's Unabridged* between *ensorcell*

(what desire does to the brain)

    and *ensphere*—

what we think the head does to the spirit,

    though it might be the opposite—

the soul ensphering the body, the body

    meant to contain only what it could, a tenth,

of its guiding spirit, the rest

    streaming continually out—

the way light illuminates the lampshade and spills over the edges—

    but the word that stops my search is *ensoul*:

where did they find a being without one—a body, a bleak house

    waiting for that happy family of four?

Is it something slipped

    to the baby just before birth or in the slap just after

(the soul so deeply asleep it needs slapping awake)?

To endow with a soul awes me:

perhaps we're every color and shape of soulless vase

    awaiting water and blossom, and only a saintly few so graced,

but what stops my breath is

    to take or put into the soul,

as if the soul were a receptacle that could be filled

    with anything—daisies or roses, trash or ashes. I'd want

to be exquisitely careful what I allowed in there—

    when I think of it, I've had or assumed

scant control over what I allowed in

    or what's been tossed in my soul.

I have been the epergne I was looking for—

    that ornamental silver stand or crystal dish

meant to put food in or take food from—

    I have not done what the poets have done

which is to give objects or words a soul—a variation

    on idolatry—or a form of grace?

What the poets have done is to give death

    a soul, which I have not done not out of humility, but fear:

once death has soul, if death *is* the mother of beauty

    what mercies or cruelties are not possible?

Living Without

Out is never content to stay there.
It's not enough that we're in it,
but out must be in us.
Our house in the woods, the wood of our house;
the ants, bees, wasps, flies and mice in our house,
the cold in our house,
the birds we feed at our window.
The lines of separation blur and dissolve until
I can no longer tell where the woods stop
and I begin, the difference between
the feeding birds and my own hungry hands.
We are in the territory of the wind,
and it lets us know, constantly
shifting, clearing its throat,
muttering to itself—and under cover of night—
pushing at, and sometimes shoving
the house an inch closer to somewhere
or an inch further away,
until one warm night in March
when we open the bedroom door
and watch the curtain arch into the room,
slim, and grey in the dark,
the wind fiercely, exultantly, in at last,
and never more other than now.
Perhaps it's the suddenness of the change
I cannot accept.
All month the snow has melted reluctantly,
almost invisibly, its white-knuckled hands
guarding the secrets it has kept all winter—
and now, this fierce warm wind in the night.
I close the door and pull the blankets up to my chin—
but the wind is in.

Rain

One part curbed, one part spilling over,
I am the gutter's reckless water,

the smeared dark rainbows of oil
adorning newly glamorous spit-shined

streets ribboned with red and white lights,
the drowned asphalt riven by the tires'

consistent hiss, streets housing drugstores,
dance-clubs, Jehovah's Witnesses,

and jugglers. G-men, con men, claustrophobics,
commitment-phobics—whole lives

lived traveling, or alone in one house.
I am the shattered multi-colored

shadows of cars reflected in the streets'
black mirror. I'm the lingering sting

of your fist striking the table, your throat's
unbearable constriction, your abruptly indrawn

breath—embrace me. I'm all that stands between you
and a yellowing stack of Sunday travel sections'

slow accretion of dust, a thousand
indistinguishable Sundays spent watching

the sunlight slip across the sinktop—
I am the trip to Brazil you've promised yourself:

that midnight rumba in Rio de Janeiro with
a woman in red, the slow boat down the Amazon—

I promise nothing, and everything:
I am the woman you should have married

offering you another chance, the next
slick kiss landing firmly on your lips.

Y

We began by trying to draw a line
between two points—but missed

the second point—drawing
a line straight to infinity, that dread number

discovered suddenly at twelve or so,
when you learn you've been lied to: that

there are numbers below zero. Numbers
above a bezillion. Numbers so cold

they must be handled with gloves
as thick as oven mitts, so hot

they must be viewed through welding glass.
You're aware now, of things which weigh

less than nothing: grief, a black hole
subtracting the universe from itself.

Things which make *you* weigh less
than nothing: the lack of gravity

called joy. You're aware of the earth's
edge, of being too close to it,

feel betrayed not to have been told
about this chasm

you could have stumbled into any time.
Now, as you try to grasp the concept

of infinity, to hold onto this greased
pig of an idea, you understand

that you are falling already, that
you have begun your life's work—

that perpetual revision of every belief, continual
admission of ignorance.

The more you know, the less you comprehend. Is this
where apprehension begins?

Today, we think we've found an answer
to this dreadful unending line, curve it

into a circle, stopping at this mountaintop
where we began our romance.

A perfect movie finish, at last, a tidy end
to all our questions. But near the hike's mid-point,

we've changed our minds about circles:
no further attempts at friendship.

Forty feet from the summit, we part,
tracing a "Y" on the mountain's furrowed brow.

On Principle

In the field after rain,
    ice like resin, or reason
so clear I can't see
    on what I stand—
though I can see
    three feet below—a freeze
so swift it caught the yellow
    grasses, some combed
and some not, bent left
    and right, some standing
still and some mid-
    swoon, but every stalk's
last protest recorded
    in tiny bubbles
that began to rise
    then froze in transit.
This afternoon
    the lowering sun
lights that world—
    all its gold grasses,
its bubbles and
    fissures and caves—
with gold light,
    the grass returning
gold with interest
    or seeming to,
and I've forgotten
    how cold my ears
without my hat, my
    hands without gloves—
or nearly,
    standing on thin
invisible ice,
    or nearly.

The Point

The point being when a star dies
   the light continues for years
yet illuminates nothing here,
   not the cottage edging the lakeshore,
which from this distance
   is not lit, but marked, by its light;
the same way the firefly suddenly starring
   my windshield illuminates neither
the dark highway or splattered window,
   but only its own small deathplace.
I observe how its light
   doesn't vanish or dim immediately,
but shrinks slowly, as if receding.
   My sadness for the firefly blooms larger and darker
than I can fathom, drawing the no I'd use
   for human loss, but dwindling with realization
at the cry's end. The point being
   that the light lives on…
and that it disappears.

Edward

I think I told you once
why I loved your name:
moving nearer Ed.

Now, I've moved away,
and I'm still moving,
the wake widening between us,
or the runway lengthening—
it doesn't matter...
whatever was between us blurs—
only the vehicle I'm in is distinct:

the clear arc of the windshield,
and the long blue curve of the fender
as I move onward, at the speed of thought.

Something About Desire

Something I wanted
to say about desire,
but I've lost my grip
on the feeling or words—
something about the day
we finally made it to Point Lobos—
so eager to show you its crags
and hollows, its luminous
Jade Bay, surf throwing itself against
invulnerable cliffs, the continuous
fountain of spray.

Something that connects up
to any one languid weekend
at the lake, late and missed meals,
Swiss chocolate, English tea and jam—

something about how we and the storm
arrived simultaneously. Instead of storming,
we were stormed—blown nearly off
the point's arthritic knuckle, bent double,
eyes streaming, lashed by stinging sand.
Soaked seconds out of the car—
we gave up and lay laughing
in the puddling seats.

Something about being back
at the hotel room with separate beds,
back to *just friends*,
the teasing ending abruptly
with your good-night kiss, the sudden
space next to me, quickly cooling sheets.

Something about a day—memory of a day
which had nothing to do with desire—
and therefore, everything.

What Happens

The stairs are there every moonless two a.m.,
same as they are in light. It happens
when my legs and feet know this,
while my mind seems to sleep.

My mind wants to know
how I do it, why I don't
stop, turn on the light—
but my unwondering feet
descend calmly in darkness,
each cell with its memory of stairs
and stars—each sure of its aim and intent
to pull me smoothly along—
unwilling, inept, and unsure.

Over My Head

In the dream is a box
too heavy to lift, which
I must lift over my head.
Something is written on the sides
of the box, blurred as if by
distance or emotion,
and it is filled with books.
Books and more books. What
is in the books? Stories, poems,
lessons; what is in the books
is words. I have a load of words
too heavy to bear and with this
I must be satisfied, or *of* this
I must divest myself—
I am unsure. I take the books out
and put them back, packing them
differently each time. I fling one
from me—words fly like confetti,
fall everywhere, sticking to places
I don't want them stuck.
When I brush my cheek, several words
flutter attractively earthward.
I stay to admire their descent,
so unlike my own.
The way they glide the air.
Their clumsy aerobatics.
Falling, or flying?
I am still not sure, not
like my waking self.

Fog

Imagine falling victim to lost names and forgotten clothing…
  then imagine the opposite—to remember *everything*:
each useless bit of information, each insult, humiliation, cramp,

bruise, burn—you get the idea—
  so a major part of our brain's function must be forgetting:
all the nevers I've said to you, the strawberry jam,

wheat toast and coffee I might have had for breakfast June 8, 1982—
  a day on which no one I loved died or was born;
day on which events must have busied themselves with other lives.

Perhaps I'll forget how, on the mountains this morning,
  the fog looks like an unmade bed
or a careless shawl warming the hill's green shoulders,

and how the self-help books
  would deplore my giving us a *fourth* chance—
the exact flavor of the *canard à l'orange*,

one night at your friend's flat in Geneva, *cresson avec
  une vinaigrette à l'huile de noisette*…I'll forget,
as I forgot the rough wings of your eyebrows under my lips;

your hair's dark water cooling my fevered hands;
  your hands' tantalizing journey—remember
how the fog looked like an unmade bed?

Now, it's a boiling cauldron; a wedding dress
  hastily discarded; a torn curtain alternately
rising and falling with the leisurely, lilac-scented air.

I'd forgotten how it suddenly hides
  or reveals, the veil unexpectedly punctuated by sugar maple,
weathered barn, red pine, or greying elm,

the café where I dined with a friend last summer—
   let me forget how she died;
let the curtain descend on that scene.

Bless all I have gained and lost: delight and grief,
   embarrassing mistakes and appalling minutiae. Bless
my brain's stubborn remembrance, its inexplicable forgetting.

Here & Then

How strange, to be in two
places at once, or in two times. This
Cambridge Sunday afternoon, *That's
me*, he says—here, sitting with his
tailbone hanging off the couch's
edge, friends and Sunday paper
spread around the living room,

and there, on the radio, playing
bass guitar—no three places—
somewhere, *live*, on stage, recording
the song for radio broadcast—
four—his mind remembering
how he felt that day, the place
he played, so he's in none

of those places, really, nor here
now, either. And me—I'm five,
giggles rising in the Santa Barbara
air like soap bubbles—
my uncles tickling me—
delight so lucid
I can return to it anytime without
going anywhere—I think.

I am paddling a friend's canoe
across a Vermont pond at dusk…
and you? Are you where your body,
or your mind is? Only space and time
between us and the fear
we're floating aimlessly
through a fathomless universe—or worse,
circling the same memories the way this dog
turns several times around
before lying down at last, to sleep.

What Was Saved

Kneeling in the ruined house
as if in too-late a prayer,

my lover and I sorted
through what once was mine.

Another day of salvage, learning
what can and cannot be saved.

Not the clothes burned off
the hangers, but some of the ones

in drawers: socks,
my first bikini brought to light—

lighting my lover's eyes—
my sooty hands ripping the suit

I'd grown too large or embarrassed for—
his dismay and my shame, a marriage,

acrid as the soot misting all the fire
owned—the books' blackened tops

and spines a penance,
for all the reading I did—

or didn't do? It was years
and a continent away when finally

I found the chemical sponge
to erase the soot's dark claim.

Did I finally undo what that evening—
or those years—had done,

swept away like those clinging
black eraser crumbs?

The books are mine again,
though still marked, as I,

by fire's sign.
Two days after I worried

I could lose my poems to fire,
I found them (browned around the edges

as if twice signed, intact),
found myself freed

of all but language and memory,
to rise from ash, and begin again.

The Way Back

Two hands on the wheel,

one hand on the wheel,

the bent knee's ache,

the stopping, or not stopping,

the singing to the self,

the self wordless, tires

greeting the familiar

gravel, the apartment

waiting like a woman, one

I've been neglectful of—

no, it's the woman waiting

like the apartment

I'll soon fill with my music,

my elaborate human noise—

it's the woman singing

to the self—it's the apartment

I've been neglectful of—

did I say who was singing?

Then, Not

The door, full of stubbornness

    tonight, heaving reluctantly

open, and requiring an extra shove

    to shut. Your lights

white, then red, then not.

    I bend to turn the resisting lock—

remembering—first, adjust the knob

    clockwise, counterclockwise,

and clockwise again, the silence

    overwhelmed by all my rattling,

then not. The doorknob, sticky

    from maple syrup this morning…

for a moment holds my hand—

    and for a moment, I can't let go.

Red Glove

The red glove in the road
   this morning, moved
to the tree this afternoon,

angled so it seems to be waving
   hello, something cheerful,
or cautionary—

like a cop waving me on
   past disaster. This morning
I straddled the glove with my wheels

without thought
   or connection, my life,
unlike yours, still marked only

by minor loss. Some mishap,
   little or large, led
to the glove being left

in the road, someone's
   care hung it
in the tree. That's what

we do here to aid recovery,
   placing hat or glove
on mailbox, window ledge

or parking meter—
   a strictly local
lost and found. Perhaps

you'll return and find
   the bright glove
in the bare tree, a signal

like the return
  of red-winged blackbirds;
the beech shedding last year's

translucent leaves. I imagined
  I would die driving—nobody
was supposed to die now.

The effect of your
  absence, something
that can't be measured

or qualified by any paradigm
  I know, like the effect
of the glove in the tree,

like subatomic entities, it
  can be defined as a particle,
and also as a wave.

If physics are right, you've
  only been changed, not lost, if
we're whole in every part,

and all part of the whole—
  you're everywhere.
Between seeing the glove

in the road this morning
  and the sign in the tree tonight,
I learned of your death.

Will there be a sign
  to tell me if you finally
find ease and comfort?

The Music We Travel By

Geneva makes them
double-length, busses
that bend in the middle

at every turn, the two halves
joined by fragile accordion,
bellows fixed

by a spinning wheel,
a counter-weight
or counter-spin preserving

this delicate marriage
from the journey's constant
shocks, as the bus turns,

the accordion folds,
and the wheel cants
like a deciding compass

as the two halves strain
toward each other,
then away, playing the tune

we travel by, music
I almost hear.
You're riding the bus's

loose end, the one that might
go flying off anytime
without the engine's guide;

while my luggage
bumps against me,
hindering my balance

on the wheel: my
not-quite-falling dance
at every corner as we turn

to our travels
together, as the wheel
turns me now

a little toward you,
now a little away—
toward you, and away.

Whose Fragile Lips

I feel your watching while I wash dishes—
gratitude, admiration—or regret?

First the glasses, whose fragile lips I trace
with a lover's hands: glass too thin

at the rims, bottoms too round not to slip
my soapy grasp, though I keep thinking

I'll invent a better grip. Do I press too hard—
or is the glass too frail?

I can not hold it gently enough.
Under my strength I see it breaking

like before, opening, and reopening
the white crescent moon of my early injury.

Just seven stitches in a body's life
of injuries, but I remember every time

I ease my hand into the soapy glass,
grateful, for each reprieve.

It's not the severity, but the nature
of the injury, skin so thin there, bone

so near—the idea, that I do this to myself.
How shall I seek to embrace my weakness,

now I know everything I will ever believe
about strength, or love, is wrong?

Edelweiss

Beloved of lovers, I
have beheld them
in their spiky silver collars
nodding defiantly at snow.
Bring some for me, she says
wistfully, when I describe them
over long-distance, but I know
of no flowers I can bring her,
least of all these—
so delicate, after all—
that will not weep
in my hands.

The Name of the Mold

Every spring there's a moment before blight,
before mildew on phlox or the latticework

left by appetite on viburnum and lilac and rose,
before the creeping yellow slime mold

appears suddenly after rain on the pine mulch,
and puffs itself up and attacks the foxglove—

then dries and flattens and browns as if
it never meant to eat Maine.

There's a moment when all the leaves
are shiny and green without blemish,

when I think a benevolent god will grant me
one summer without affliction.

Am I fallen because I've failed the garden
or does the garden fail because I'm fallen—

or is it a great temerity in me to think
I have anything at all to do with it?

We've eaten the apple and the first thing
we think we know is whose fault it is.

Sure

I've a reputation for being sure-
minded—it's what I tell myself I am.

Something I somehow misunderstood
as a virtue, a mantra I've used for comfort:

I've been called numb as a pounded
thumb, but never unsure. Sure

I know what I want, sure-footed,
sure-handed, sure the first time

he placed his finger in the "V"
of my satin green pajamas

and asked to see my tan-line,
sure the last time, when he murmured,

"I remember these..." Two break-ups
and reconciliations have taken the edge

off my surety, and I've begun to be
a doubter: is the sideways glance

he's sliding me plot, or invitation?
Just how worthy is this canoe—how wet

is the water, in which direction
shall we paddle? I'm not sure

what the dusty green of this pond, warm
as pee this summer, covers.

I'd guess the bottom's muddy and riddled
with water weeds, but the depth, I suspect,

is shallow. *Are you sure you want to know?*
he says. *Sure,* I say, *is what I've built my life on.*

Against Entropy

Truly, it's the waning
of the moon,
and the too crowded
sky requiring effort—
you call that a bear?—
starry disarray
I'm itching to arrange.
How seeing must I be
to draw new constellations?
All my life tilts toward this,
all my desire is design—
is it the chair that requires warming,
or the ass that desires shape?

Serious

I thought it was the end of the world—something I always knew I'd see
in my lifetime—it's just been that kind of a life: always the untied

shoelace to trip on, the split seam over the one pair of panties patterned
with little hearts. I'm hoping next time, I'll get a serious life. Something

really big: Mother Teresa, or Jesus. This time around I'm just Someone's
little cosmic joke, maybe even my own: I thought I'd live one life

just for laughs. But I was telling about the world's end at a London theater,
how in a love scene's tender midst, the room began to shake, the rumbling

turning to muted roar, echoing the lovers' shuddering progress,
so I thought they'd climax together in one last earth-rending explosion

of noise and light, then collapse into some final dark completion. *Yes,
this is how I want to go*, I thought, happy voyeur, true child of the video-age.

Who wants the risk of STD's, actual flesh touching flesh, perilous
exchange of bodily fluids, or the prophylactic alternatives, gloved

hands, sex reduced to a dry rubbing, the indignant squeak
of new sneakers on tiled floor. The rumbling stopped, catching me

in mid-cheer. The tube, of course, was underneath:
trains careering through smutty tunnels—a chambered nautilus

the city rests its obese, ancient weight upon. Nervous,
impatient suits scurry along its deserted subterranean corridors

or shove through rapid, silent swarms of commuters, descending
urine-scented stairs to wait on grimy platforms—avoid the slow-moving

homeless, the upturned hands. Neckhairs rising each time a train's
blinding eye thunders from the tunnel's black wound and shrieks

to a halt, they hurry over that dark interstice between
train door and platform, heeding the disembodied, omniscient voice

intoning, "Mind—the—gap. Mind—the—gap." The suits move fast,
and they want fast trains out of that netherworld. What's the distance

between the fast and the slow—or between us? How little a tug would it take
to snap your life's fragile grace, and find yourself in my place, out there somewhere

tripping over your shoelace, applauding your own dimly lit performance, my
rueful chuckle just now escaping your tightening throat?

Photo of the Artist With Chainsaw

Watch-arm forward,
the hand with chainsaw
back, he's heading out
the right side of the frame,

paused an instant
in determination.
The paper birch beside him's
an epiphany of yellow, his

attention's fixed on some
other point: black walnut,
basswood, butternut.
He hears sirens singing

the names of trees
he'll cut, then carve,
of the birds he'll create.
He wants to give himself

wholly to something, not
like he gave himself
to women, to the bottle
and needle, no,

just this once,
he thinks, he'll give himself
to something beautiful
and clear and final. Just

this once give himself
to something with
no holding back—something
to turn him soulside-out,

like jade green blown
Venetian glass. He'll sing
an opera, dance the tango.
He'll remember finally,

all the names he's forgotten,
and answer to his own:
Edward Hopkins, wildlife
artist, willing to travel.

Peony

I touch her feather-
light all over her
body for a long time

as peace and
pleasure flicker
alternately over

her face. My lips
flower against her
in exactly the way

that a peony
opens itself to sun.
Tomorrow,

as the rose-like odor
rises in the air,
I realize too late

I have trodden
precisely
a discarded peony.

What lover flung
it with what haste
from what window?

It's a many-windowed
residence and I
am too close to it:

to see it all
I must tip my head
backward till it hurts.

One With It

Just enough snow to cheer,
to give every shape
definition, each dark outline
thinly visible in muted noon light:
the dark branches and white branches,
nude or fog-cloaked, equally graceful
in their reaching—
the law of growth toward light,
mirror of their roots' dark reach—
not toward dark so much as within and one with it;
the river farms' sheared-off, orderly corn rows;
fog rising from melting snow like smoke;
rain pelting earth, road and windshield alike—
and I am not weary
of its metronome, of its damp trickling
through my hair at every stop,
nor am I weary of the snow's steamy breath,
its white fire burning the human-made
and the nature-made
with picture-perfect equanimity
and equality.

A Kind of Music

Name the things
    the body does fast naturally—

sneeze—(so dangerous
    it requires blessing), injure,

or submit to injury—if we had time
    to think, we wouldn't do it.

Consider that "fast" means
    held securely in one place

as well as being a measure
    of the speed of motion,

that "quick" means alive
    as well as fast, that "dead"

is the final measure
    of the lack of motion, so speed

must be a measure
    of life, and the quality of life

a measure of speed,
    so if you're in the check-out

line at the grocery
    (remembering that "checking out"

is slang for dying),
    and the line's not fast

in the sense of moving
    at an acceptable speed, that's life

threatening, and reason enough
    for ire—and ire, a catalyst

for rousing us to action—
    as is desire, which keeps us

all in motion—as does
    thwarted desire—

which leads us back to ire...
    Consider that music is used

to rouse as well as soothe,
    that no music is made

without motion, that the body,
    hearing music, is moved

to motion (the heart,
    to emotion); that speed

is a kind of music—
    the music we most desire

to dance to—dance, dance
    until our feet shall fail.

Dinner Party

after Mark Halliday

Well, it's me of course—completely me—
it almost, but not quite, *screams* me.

You could say it sings me, but I wouldn't—
that's really too Whitman, too self-conscious. Basically,

it's just the kind of person I am. All
of the furniture is simply limned, neutral,

and mono-toned (tastefully, but
discreetly textured) so you notice the art,

and photographs, the extensive collection
of books, and the vase of flowers, which

might happen to be standing on the coffee table,
which is really a hope chest my brother made for me

when we were kids—I'm that sentimental, that
cared for—and that's crucial to me—

crucial that you know. There's the three-tiered
oak magazine holder my mother made

in high school, back when girls weren't allowed
to take "woodshop," and she formed her own

all-girls wood-working club, so you can see
how my things aren't just *things* like other people's,

but have meaning and stand for something; how
there's a story to everything—

did I mention I'm a writer?
There's the pine plant stand an ex-boyfriend

(who happens to be an artist) made me, but
most of all there is the wall of bookcases

I built myself, right here in this living room—
mid-winter, with borrowed power tools,

and well below zero outside—my first real winter,
(you know I'm originally from California, one of the few

actual natives). I'd never built shelves before, but
somehow managed to do a pretty good job, n'est-ce pas?

(A little French I picked up from my Swiss boyfriend—
it slays me when he talks French—like when we're in bed,

I mean, I get goosebumps all over, you wouldn't
think such a good-looking guy would be so good

in bed, would you?). I really could have been an artist or
an interior decorator or a gourmet chef—you know?

I mean—if you're going to do something, why not
do it well? In fact, I tend to do everything well, though

it's mainly because I'm careful not
to attempt things I'm pretty sure I'd flop at—

like karaoke—definitely the most humiliating
experience of my life, I mean, I can't sing worth

beans, and I know this, so I really didn't
want to get up there, but they made me—

can you imagine?
I don't know how I got talked into that, anyway.

Well, as I was saying, it's small but charming
(people always say that), and cozy. I like to feel people

are comfortable in my place—I try to create that
kind of atmosphere—tidy, but not obsessive

or compulsive, not like you could eat off the floor—
I always say a little dirt's good for you, builds up your

immunities. Notice the pine floors, and exposed beams?
That's really *in* now, but I got this place

way before that. And there are a couple photos of my boyfriend
who happens to be incredibly handsome, I mean he's not a type

I usually go for, you understand—just a couple of photographs
strategically, but not obviously placed,

just prominent enough that you'd ask "Who's *that*?"
I'd answer quite casually, even a bit clipped, "Boyfriend."

—just the one word by itself so you'd have no hint of whether
he's a current or ex-boyfriend, and it would be completely

(but subtly) clear that I could dump even this unbelievably
handsome man without a qualm. I'm that self-confident.

Separations

Oxygen in, carbon dioxide out,
my skin cooled by the air,
the air warmed by my body—

shall I call these borrowed gasses mine
or shall I call myself a creature of air,
earthbound so briefly—

my bones turning to earth,
my flesh giving up
its various elements

and melting into air
in what might be called
an ascension.

Satisfaction

Probably you're one of the few
people who can say they're
satisfied—no, I mean *really*

satisfied—I don't mean people
who try to convince you or
themselves, or make lists of how,

I mean just being, and being
quiet about it, so you can see
how calm, centered, and self

aware you are, how accepting of life's
quirks and surprises,
how nothing surprises you

because you're truly satisfied,
take joy in small things—joy's
taking you for an indefinite (or

do I mean definite?) ride, joy's
your best girlfriend wearing
a red floppy hat, driving

a swish convertible,
and singing with the radio,
your hair streaming back

from your faces and everything
in soft focus, not that you don't
see clearly, I mean life is just

like that for you, and seems lucky
but is really the result
of your hard work and great

attitude, except—
you know how sometimes
in Boston, in early spring,

with trees all either leafing out
or blooming, how you realize,
again, that there *are*

trees in Boston and people
smiling—*really* smiling,
and you feel a kind of

connection—a feeling of fullness,
but also of loss?
Or you think about the homeless

and how cushy your life is
in comparison or how there's war,
famine, suffering all over

and you should remember
to be more grateful than you are
even though your nearly perfect

boyfriend's commitment-shy,
or you couldn't afford that new
blue dress to dance in, but,

hey, you've got legs to dance on,
the body that would
look nice in the dress, the finger

that would look right in the ring.
So you're grateful,
even if what you don't have

is more real
than what you do.

Fusion

A summons, it had all

    the sex and soul of Soul but wasn't,

nor Jazz nor Rock nor Latin—of course

    it was composed and performed

by souls, and summoned them—

    soul of the electric violin,

the composer playing it, the street

    full of people he played it in,

keyboard, drums, percussion,

    the passion with which he played—

clearly he composed it—the violinist

    sporting the black "muscle T," tattooed

shoulder, shaved head—his lips

    in the shape of a kiss

not meant for anyone,

    shape of an answer

to a question we hadn't asked,

    music in the shape

of a solo, solo,

    the shape of a soul—

when, finally,

    we learn the answers

will we have forgotten

    all the questions, the soul

a mystery in plain sight?

Belief

It's the sudden waking—almost electroshock—
that sensation of having lofted several inches
off the bed, then fallen: the spirit slipping
back into the body after a night's journey.

So terrifying—your first fear and your last—
what is it about falling
that attracts? The urge, unconquerable,
to creep up to the cliff's edge, your recurring
dream of falling, but never landing.

Lying on the ground looking up,
you grew dizzy with falling skywards, your
whole body straining gratefully against
the dank, solid earth, which you inhaled,
then kissed surreptitiously upon rolling over,

when you knew, just for an instant,
you too could zoom wingless over any map, any history
or prediction—the places and times all blurring together
or leaping into focus as you hover for a closer look,
or speed away, *except there'd be no away*—

in those terrifying milliseconds of belief
before you shake your head
and put out both hands to ward off the awful burden,
you realize you too could walk on water.

Acknowledgments

Grateful acknowledgment is made to the editors of the journals and anthologies who first published the following poems. The poems, sometimes in earlier versions, appeared as follows:

The Antioch Review: "Something About Desire"; *Cincinnati Poetry Review*: "Living Without"; *Colorado Review*: "Edelweiss," "Then, Not"; *Contemporary New England Poetry* (University Press of New England): "Red Glove," "Living Without"; *Harvard Review*: "One"; *Interim*: "A Kind of Music," "Peony," "The Way Back"; *Isle: Interdisciplinary Studies in Literature & Environment*: "Separations"; *Mid-American Review*: "Epergne"; *MiPo Magazine* (online journal): "Here & Then"; *Poetry Northwest*: "The Point"; *Potpourri*: "Edward"; *Prairie Schooner*: "Over My Head," "Sure," "Serious," "Dinner Party," "Satisfaction," "The Music We Travel By"; *Puerto del Sol*: "Whose Fragile Lips"; *Seneca Review*: "Fog"; *The Spoon River Poetry Review*: "Y." "Satisfaction" was also published in *The Maine Poets: An Anthology of Verse* (Down East Books).

"In Principle" is dedicated to Aimee and Don. "Red Glove" is for Lynda. To my teachers and to Anne Marie, Catherine, Ellen and Jocelyn for their aid in shaping these poems, and to family and friends for their long and unflagging faith and encouragement: my love and thanks.

April Ossmann has published her poetry widely in journals including *Colorado Review* and *Harvard Review,* and in the anthologies *Contemporary New England Poetry* and *The Maine Poets: An Anthology of Verse.* She won the *Prairie Schooner* Readers' Choice Award for ten poems published in the summer 2000 issue. She is executive director of Alice James Books, and has taught creative writing and literature courses at Lebanon College and at the University of Maine at Farmington.